Illustrated

DEVOTIONAL

FOR

Women

CAROLYN LARSEN

CHRISTIAN ART
PUBLISHERS

You Are Pure and Blameless

An ink pen leak or grape juice spill means a stain quickly develops. A stain that's nearly impossible to get out. Even after scrubbing, a slight indication of it often remains.

If it weren't for what Jesus did, your heart would be permanently stained by your sins. You could apologize until you're blue in the face but if Jesus hadn't died for your sin, it wouldn't matter. Your sin demanded a price ... a blood sacrifice. That's exactly what Jesus gave for you. He died for your sins, paying the price for them, making a way for you to have a personal relationship with God.

Because of Jesus' sacrifice, you stand before God clean and pure. Your sins are forgiven. Your heart has no stain. Who are you in Christ? You are His beloved pure, clean and blameless child, because of the sacrifice of Jesus, who loves you with abandon.

He came to deliver us from our sinful dispositions, and create in us pure hearts, and when we have Him with us it will not be hard for us. Then the service of Christ will be delightful.

DWIGHT L. MOODY

12/26/

You Are Salt

Salt is common. It can be found in every home. In fact, it's so common that you might even say it's nothing special. So, why does Jesus say that you are salt? Think about the uses for salt— salt flavors foods. It purifies. It preserves. It is used for binding (I know that's a weird one).

Your saltiness is your committed life to Christ. Living for Him, even when it's not popular. Each time you obey and love it is like a grain of salt dropped into the lives of those around you. You preserve the evidence of a life lived for Him. Your obedience will possibly motivate others to obey Him, making life better for all. Salt binds together proteins in food, making them stick together. By living for Christ, you encourage others to know Him and by discipling them, you can help bind them to Jesus.

If we are to better the future we must disturb the present.

CATHERINE BOOTH

You Are Christ's Ambassador

You are Christ's ambassador, but what does an ambassador do? An ambassador lives in a foreign land and builds relationships with people so that they may know and understand the person she represents.

How are you Christ's ambassador? You live in a foreign land; a world that doesn't know Him. As you build relationships people get a glimpse of what Jesus is like by how you live. Make it a positive glimpse by making it your goal to be a sincere example of His kindness, compassion and peace. Be careful to guard your words and reign in quick judgments.

Are these things easy? Not always. But consider what a privilege it is that He called you to be His ambassador. He trusts you to represent Him by your example of His love and care. Your words, your attitudes, your actions as Christ's ambassador can draw people to Him.

God is looking for those with whom He can do the impossible —
what a pity that we plan only the things that we can do by ourselves.
A.W. TOZER

You Are Unchained

Opinions and judgments race through the social media world. If you let any of those things settle in your heart, you will struggle to feel any kind of freedom. However, Jesus says you are free.

Paul was reminding his readers that they are free from the legalities of the Old Testament. They no longer need to make animal sacrifices. They no longer must worry about the rules the Pharisees insisted they live by. Their only focus was to obey Jesus and live the way He taught. They were now free from the man-made rules of the past and should be careful not to fall back into them.

You are free too, from the sin that controlled your past, from rules that are man-made, not God-ordained. You are free to become the glorious person God made you to be! He already sees you that way!

It is a tremendous freedom to get rid of all
self-consideration and learn to care about only one thing—
the relationship between Christ and ourselves.

OSWALD CHAMBERS

WE KNOW, DEAR BROTHERS AND SISTERS, THAT

GOD LOVES YOU

AND HAS CHOSEN YOU

TO BE HIS OWN PEOPLE.

1 Thessalonians 1:4

You Are Chosen

Remember gym class when the teacher chose team captains and let them take turns choosing their teams. If you weren't especially athletic you may have been one of the last ones chosen or even ended up being assigned to a team. Not a good feeling. Being chosen makes you feel wanted, needed … special.

Here's an amazing story of being chosen—God has chosen you to be a part of His own family. You did nothing to deserve His choosing. You don't have to have any special skill or training to be chosen. God chooses you simply because He loves you. He has a plan for your life and the presence of His Holy Spirit will teach and guide you as your faith in Him grows deeper.

How blessed you are that you are chosen! You belong to God and that changes everything for the better!

We did not happen to be—we were chosen by God to exist.

MOTHER ANGELICA

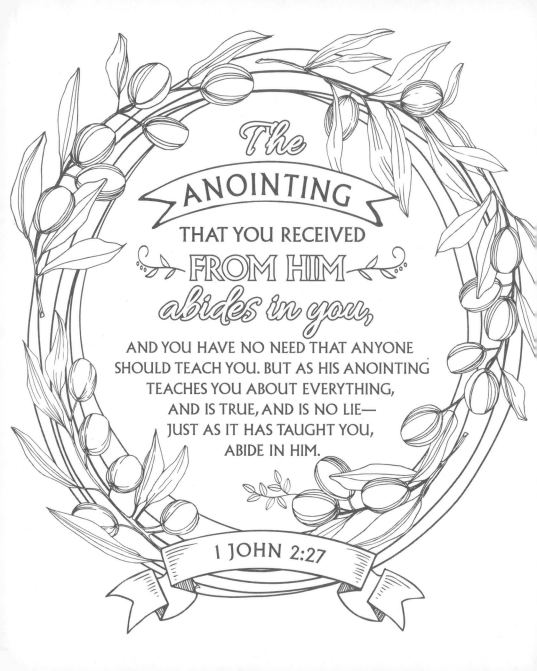

The
ANOINTING
THAT YOU RECEIVED
FROM HIM
abides in you,
AND YOU HAVE NO NEED THAT ANYONE
SHOULD TEACH YOU. BUT AS HIS ANOINTING
TEACHES YOU ABOUT EVERYTHING,
AND IS TRUE, AND IS NO LIE—
JUST AS IT HAS TAUGHT YOU,
ABIDE IN HIM.

1 JOHN 2:27

You Are Anointed

What does it mean to be anointed? This verse speaks of the anointing of the Holy Spirit. God's Spirit lives in you and God promises that He will teach you about everything. That doesn't mean there is not value in human teachers, but the Spirit guides you to recognize God's truth. His anointing helps you discern real truth from the many voices shouting false truth.

Some historians speculate that the practice of anointing began when shepherds would pour oil on their sheep's heads to keep insects from crawling into their ears and killing them. The oil made the wool slippery so the bugs slid away. Think about that … their ears were protected. The Spirit's anointing and teaching protects you from the words of a false teacher as He guides you to God's truth. Pay attention to the Spirit. He is a gift to you.

Earthly wisdom is doing what comes naturally.
Godly wisdom is doing what the Holy Spirit compels us to do.

CHARLES STANLEY

IN ALL THESE THINGS WE ARE MORE THAN CONQUERORS THROUGH HIM WHO LOVED US.

ROMANS 8:37

You Are a Conqueror

You will come out on top! You are a conqueror, winner, victor, top of the hill! Nothing ... absolutely nothing can defeat you. Of course, it may not feel that way sometimes. But, because you belong to Jesus and He loves you so very much, it's true. You're not just a "barely squeaked through" conqueror—you have more than conquered. Your victory breaks records! Because of Jesus, you come out way on top! Nothing can defeat you. No job is too big. No relationship too difficult. No challenge too frightening.

So, when life starts getting you down, fight discouragement by remembering Who you belong to. Remember that your power comes from Jesus through His overwhelming, powerful love for you. The victory may not come today but your trust in Jesus' conquering power will grow your faith deeper. Claim victory and watch to see how He brings it to pass!

God doesn't call us to be comfortable. He calls us to trust Him so completely that we are unafraid to put ourselves in situations where we will be in trouble if He doesn't come through.

Francis Chan

You Are Clean

You strive for clean, don't you? You clean your body, home, windows, clothes, and dishes. You clean pretty much everything in your life. You spend a lot of time trying to achieve "clean." But there's one "clean" you can do nothing about—getting the dirt out of your heart.

You were born with the dirt of sin and it shows itself in your attitudes, behavior, and speech. All you can do about that cleanup is submit to Jesus. Give your heart to Him, acknowledge His work on the cross and receive His cleansing salvation. As you grow deeper in your relationship with God, the Holy Spirit will reveal more sins you must confess. It's hard to face the honesty of that reality but when you confess, they, too, are cleansed away by His grace and love. Jesus sees your clean heart—cleansed by His sacrificial gift.

We can be assured that each step deeper into the Lord's
Presence will reveal areas in our heart which need to be cleansed.
Do not be afraid. When the Spirit shows you areas
of sin, it is not to condemn you, but to cleanse you.

FRANCIS FRANGIPANE

Dear FRIENDS, your real home is not here on earth. You are strangers here. I ask you to keep away from all the sinful desires of the flesh. These things fight to get hold of your soul.

1 PETER 2:11

You Are a Temporary Resident

It's easy to get caught up in the struggles of this world. After all, you live here. You have to earn a living and get along with others and all of that can be tiring. The struggles those things bring drain your energy.

But the reality is that you're on this earth for a short time. This world is not your permanent home. You're heading to heaven! Keep the perspective of why you're here. Your life should be reflecting the love and personality of God to those around you. Don't get caught up in the attitudes, words, and behaviors of those who don't know Jesus. Live in such a way that others are drawn to Him. Of course, you should enjoy this life—the beauty of this earth and the love of family and friends are gifts from God. Enjoy. Celebrate. Share. But, remember, you're a temporary resident here. Heaven is your home.

My home is in heaven. I'm just traveling through this world.

BILLY GRAHAM

GOD SAVED US and called us to live a *holy life.* He did this, not because we deserved it, but because that was *His plan* from before the beginning of time—to show us *His grace* through CHRIST JESUS.

2 TIMOTHY 1:9

You Are Set Apart

To be holy means you are set apart ... moved away from the crowd ... saved for something unique. It's pretty special that you are called by God to live a holy (set apart) life but what does that mean?

Perhaps you know the saying that you are to be "in the world but not of the world." It means you live and work with people who don't know Jesus or care about living for Him. You are a part of the same world they live in ... but you're different because God's Holy Spirit lives in you, motivating you to obey Him, grow deeper in faith and serve Him. You simply can't be part of the crowd because God has called you to be set apart. You have special work to do for Him. What an honor.

Holy has the same root as wholly, it means complete.
A man is not complete in spiritual stature if all his mind,
heart, soul, and strength are not given to God.

R. J. Stewart

You Are Light

God's presence in your heart lights you from within. You shine in the dark world as a beacon of hope, kindness, love, fairness, and compassion. You are a living, breathing example of God's love and kindness and of the goodness life holds when a person falls to her knees in worship of God.

You can make a difference by being the difference—love as Jesus loves, live as Jesus teaches. Even when you're in pain, going through hard things, experiencing loss—even when it may feel like you have no light to shine ... you do. Even a small light in darkness makes a difference. The ugliness of this dark world can be overcome by the light of God's love shining through His people. Being a light in the darkness is the job Jesus has given you. Live strong. Love deep. Forgive often. Be brave. Let your light shine!

The world does not read the Bible, the world reads Christians! "You are the light of the world!"

CHARLES SPURGEON

Since we are His children, we are His heirs. In fact, together with Christ we are heirs of God's glory. But if we are to share His glory, we must also share His suffering.

Romans 8:17

You Are an Heir

God has adopted you as His child. That means you are also His heir. All that God has is yours! What an overwhelming thought. If you break it down, you will find it means things such as you inherit His forever—eternity with Him in His perfect heaven. You inherit His sinlessness—the battle you fight every day to control thoughts, actions, words, urges … gone. For eternity you will know His perfection. Your relationship with Him is unhampered by anything else. Forever you can walk and talk with your Father.

There's an old saying that blood is thicker than water. It means you stand up for and with family over any other relationship. That's true in your family relationship with God because it is the blood of Jesus that holds you together. You are an heir to all that relationship with Him means.

Think of what you are, you Christians. You are God's children;
you are joint-heirs with Christ. The "many mansions" are
for you; the palms and harps of the glorified are for you.
You have a share in all that Christ has and is and shall be.

CHARLES SPURGEON

You Are Fearless!

What scares you? Not having control of everything? Uncertainty as to what to do? A new situation? What the future holds? Those situations are scary. But, their power is destroyed by the simple fact of ... God. You belong to Him. His Spirit lives in you. Nothing surprises Him. He knows the future. He has control. He has the answers. He will guide you. He has a plan for every day of your life. You are His, so whatever life brings you can face it with the power, love, and self-control He gives you.

God wants your life to be filled with His strength so the evidence of His presence can be seen by everyone around you. The very peace you show in the face of whatever life brings will testify to His love and power in you. Your trust in God makes you fearless!

If God be our God, He will give us peace in trouble. When there is a storm without, He will make peace within. The world can create trouble in peace, but God can create peace in trouble.

THOMAS WATSON

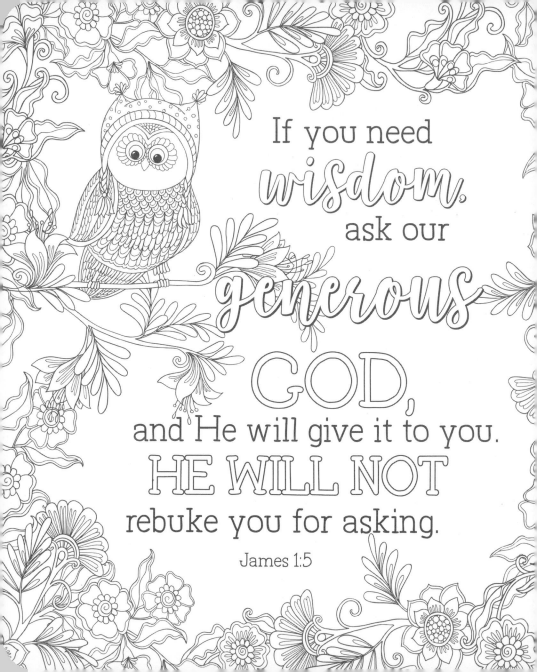

If you need *wisdom,* ask our *generous* GOD, and He will give it to you. HE WILL NOT rebuke you for asking.

James 1:5

You Are Wise

At one time or another everyone could use an extra dose of wisdom, right? In some ways, the world seems to get more confusing every day. But one thing that remains constant is God's wisdom and His generosity in sharing His wisdom with you. Maybe you're wondering how God could consider you wise when you have questions, confusions, or doubts. It's a beautiful thing that He sees you as wise because He knows that all of His wisdom is available to you and that all you have to do is ask.

Are you struggling with a decision? Ask God. Do you wonder how to stand firm in faith in this ever-changing world? Ask God. Does it seem impossible to stand firm in faith and love? Ask God. He has the answers to all those questions and a multitude more ... just ask. Then ... listen. He will give you wisdom.

Not until we have become humble and teachable, standing in awe of God's holiness and sovereignty, acknowledging our own littleness, distrusting our own thoughts, and willing to have our minds turned upside down, can divine wisdom become ours.

J. I. Packer

"Go and make disciples of all the nations,
baptizing them in the name of the Father
and the Son and the Holy Spirit."

MATTHEW 28:19

You Are a Disciple-Maker

God has a plan for your life that is bigger than you can even dream. However, His plan isn't just for you. He has a job for you to do—to make new disciples. You make disciples by first sharing His love with others, then helping new believers grow deeper and stronger in their faith. Encourage them to study God's Word and pray.

Then, as their faith grows they also have the responsibility and privilege of making disciples. Keep it going—tell people what He has done for them. Tell them of His love, His peace, His strength, and guidance. Tell them of His heaven that is theirs for eternity by accepting Jesus as Savior. Help them grow deeper in faith, learning to trust Him more, and know the power of His Spirit living in them. Being a disciple-maker is a great privilege and great responsibility.

Christianity without discipleship is
always Christianity without Christ.

DIETRICH BONHOEFFER

You Are Free

Freedom! Jesus has made you free. Free from what? Free from the reality of paying the penalty for your own sin; which would mean actually getting what you deserve. You are also free to know God—really know Him, talk with Him, commune with Him, rest in His presence, anticipate eternity with Him. You are free from condemnation. Jesus paid the price for your sin. That gives you freedom from the requirement to observe a long list of man-made rules as people who lived before Jesus died for us.

The Holy Spirit's presence in your life gives you the freedom to become the person God fully intends you to be ... a person who loves God and others with a sacrificial selflessness. You have the joyous freedom to be, to pray, to live, to give, to share who God is with others.

Either sin is with you, lying on your shoulders, or it is lying on Christ, the Lamb of God. Now if it is lying on your back, you are lost; but if it is resting on Christ, you are free, and you will be saved. Now choose what you want.

MARTIN LUTHER

WHEN I WAS A *child,*

I SPOKE AND THOUGHT AND REASONED AS A CHILD.

BUT WHEN I *grew up,*

I PUT AWAY CHILDISH THINGS.

1 CORINTHIANS 13:11

You Are Grown Up

What childish things have you put away as your faith in Jesus has grown? When you trusted Him for small things as a baby Christian and saw Him come through, your faith grew stronger. Then you trusted for bigger things. As you matured you've even been able to trust when you could see no possible way of situations being resolved. You've trusted when God's answers were not what you wanted to hear because you know that His plan is best.

Maturity in Jesus means becoming more like Him by caring and being compassionate toward others. Jesus said that the two greatest commandments are to love God and others. Part of putting away childish things means loving and trusting God and loving others as He does with fairness and consideration. The Christian life is a journey, a process of learning, trusting, and maturing. The goal is to be like Jesus.

Becoming like Christ is a long, slow process of growth.

RICK WARREN

THIS GOOD NEWS

TELLS US

HOW GOD MAKES US RIGHT

IN *His sight.*

THIS IS

ACCOMPLISHED

FROM START TO FINISH

BY FAITH.

AS THE SCRIPTURES SAY,

" IT IS THROUGH

faith THAT A

RIGHTEOUS PERSON

HAS *life.* "

Romans 1:17

You Are a Person of Faith

Living by faith sometimes can feel like stepping off a ledge into darkness. You can't see if there is any solid ground to catch you. You don't know where you're going because you can't see past the end of your nose. But you put one foot in front of the other and step out into what appears to be nothingness because you trust the One who has led you to do so. That's faith—uncompromising, unquestioning belief in God's guidance and direction. Living by faith is obedience to all God tells you in His Word and to His guidance through what His Spirit reveals to you personally.

Risk-taking faith holds you close to God and grows itself deeper and stronger as you experience His guidance and love for you. If you can't trust the One you're following, you have no faith at all. But your small first steps of faith grow deeper faith.

Faith looks not at what happens to him but at Him whom he believes.

WATCHMAN NEE

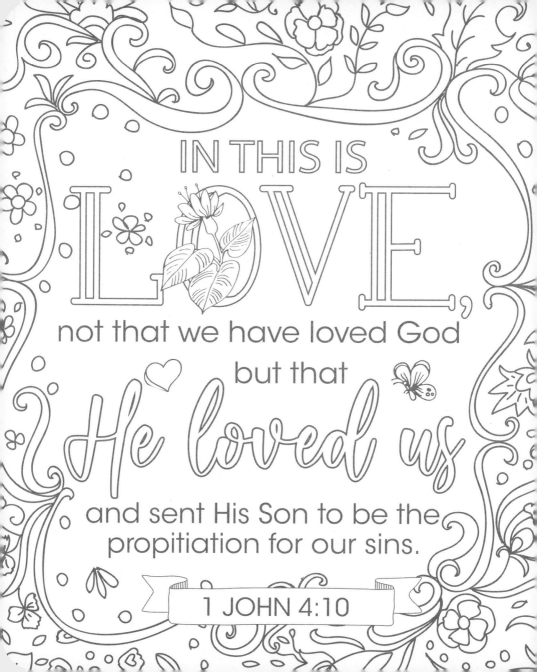

IN THIS IS
LOVE,
not that we have loved God
but that
He loved us
and sent His Son to be the
propitiation for our sins.

1 JOHN 4:10

You Are Loved

You are so incredibly, unconditionally, indescribably loved that you are seriously not even capable of understanding how big that love is. God's love for you … you … is so big that it moved Him to pay the debt for your sin. God's love for you goes beyond speaking loving words. It's bigger than wishing you well.

His love is so deep that He took action and gave His most precious beloved Son as the propitiation … the appeasement … for your sins. This is not the casual gift of a casual love. It's love that cost Him everything and gave you everything. You did nothing to earn it; could have done nothing. So when stresses and burdens weigh you down let the magnitude of this great love rise in your heart and move you to trust God more deeply and humbly every day.

God loves each of us as if there were only one of us.

St. Augustine

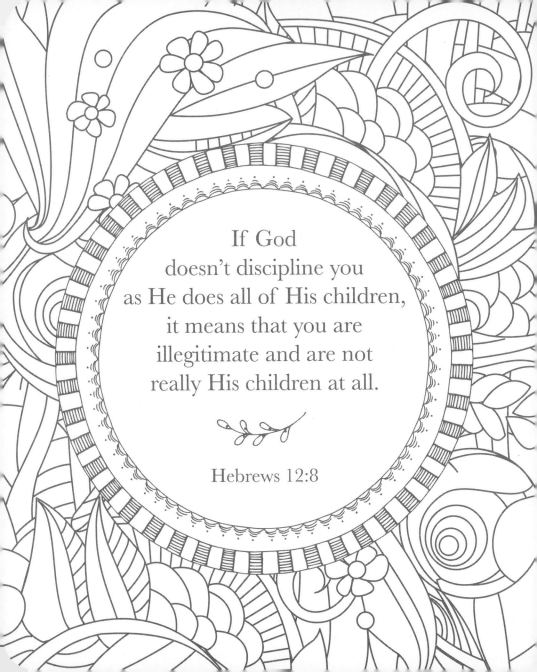

If God
doesn't discipline you
as He does all of His children,
it means that you are
illegitimate and are not
really His children at all.

Hebrews 12:8

You Are Disciplined

Discipline is the consequence of disobedient or improper behavior. However, it's not punishment. It's a teaching tool. Children are disciplined because it helps them learn to become mature, useful members of society; respectful of authority, hard workers, and law-abiding. Responsible parents take the role of discipline seriously. It's an expression of love even though it's never easy. The adage, "This hurts me more than it hurts you" may be the thought of some parents as they discipline.

When you disobey your Heavenly Father's laws or instruction, He will help you learn from them by disciplining you. This discipline comes in different ways for different people and different situations and while it may be painful, realize that it's given in love. God disciplines because He is your Father ... you are His child. If He didn't love you and care about your growth, He wouldn't discipline. Thank Him for loving you enough to discipline.

Love precedes discipline.

JOHN OWEN

BECAUSE OF HIS

glory

AND

EXCELLENCE,

He has given us

GREAT AND PRECIOUS

promises.

THESE ARE THE PROMISES THAT ENABLE
YOU TO SHARE HIS DIVINE NATURE
AND ESCAPE THE WORLD'S
CORRUPTION CAUSED BY
HUMAN DESIRES.

2 PETER 1:4

You Are an Escapee

Perhaps you've never thought of your relationship with Christ as offering you an escape. You were born with a sinful nature in a corrupt world. The pressure-filled temptation to flourish in that corruption is constant and it's impossible to defeat it on your own. Any victories are fleeting moments before being dragged back to the battle.

Jesus promises the Holy Spirit to take up residence in your heart and become your conscience to reveal God's beautifully divine nature of love and goodness. He helps you learn how to grow that nature in yourself, turning away from the world's corruption— escaping it. He warns you when you're falling back into the sinful humanness you were born with. The need for escape may be a moment-by-moment struggle or it may pop up out of nowhere and surprise you. But the route to escape is always present. God has provided a way for you.

Through salvation, our past has been forgiven, our present is given meaning, and our future is secured.

RICK WARREN

"YOU SHALL LOVE THE LORD YOUR GOD WITH ALL YOUR HEART AND WITH ALL YOUR SOUL AND WITH ALL YOUR MIND AND WITH ALL YOUR STRENGTH."

MARK 12:30

You Are All In

You must be all in with following Christ. There can be no halfway. Accepting Jesus as Savior means you are turning your back on the person you used to be and you're fully committed to knowing Him. Your heart is His. You love Him. You trust Him. Your soul, thoughts, physical strength, heart strength, mental strength are all His. God will not share you with any other gods. Being all in declares that nothing and no one is more important to you than He is.

Does it mean you are a failure if you ever have doubts or questions? Of course not. Doubts are part of faith. They stretch your faith muscle to grow it stronger. But you never give up. You never walk away because total complete love does not give up. In Christ, you are fully loved and you fully love.

Faith does not grasp a doctrine, but a heart. The trust which Christ requires is the bond that unites souls with Him; and the very life of it is entire committal of myself to Him in all my relations, and for all my needs, and absolute, utter confidence in Him as all sufficient for everything that I can require.

ALEXANDER MACLAREN

"I AM the Vine and you are the branches. Get your life from Me. Then I will live in you and you will give much fruit. You can do nothing without ME."

JOHN 15:5

You Are Fed

A vine is not just a conglomeration of branches. A plant's lifeblood is below ground, it's not even visible. The roots draw nutrition from the soil, feed it into the vine, which then dispenses it to the branches. The branches could not survive without this system.

Jesus is your vine. His life is in His Father, and from Him through Jesus comes the nutrition you need. What is this nutrition? The knowledge of God's instruction and guidance for your life. The capacity to forgive others and love as He loves. The passion to share His love and serve Him however He directs. A growing faith that yearns with an eager heart to know Him more deeply, serve Him more fully and be completely real in your relationships with others. Always keep the focus of revealing a Christ-like spirit in your daily life. Without Jesus the Vine … you can do none of this.

Abiding in Me is indispensable, for, you know it, of yourselves you can do nothing to maintain or act out the heavenly life.

ANDREW MURRAY

Do YOU not know that you are God's TEMPLE & that God's Spirit dwells in you?

1 CORINTHIANS 3:16

You Are Indwelt

The temple was the holy place where God resided. It was important to His people. It was respected and honored. Now, He lives in you so your very being is His temple. This means you are never alone. No matter if you feel deserted by others or fearful in your struggles, God is always with you. It also means that you are His witness to those others.

You may be the only Bible some people see. Those who would never darken the door of a church learn about God's love from you because He is living in you. You are His temple. Be His good representative. Respect the body God gave you. Take care of it. Be careful what you put into it. Be especially mindful of what you put into your mind and heart. Remember He's there, too. Make His temple a place that honors Him.

Those in whom the Spirit comes to live are
God's new Temple. They are, individually and
corporately, places where heaven and earth meet.
N. T. WRIGHT

WE KNOW THAT WHEN
THIS EARTHLY TENT
WE LIVE IN IS TAKEN DOWN
(THAT IS, WHEN WE DIE AND LEAVE THIS EARTHLY BODY),
WE WILL HAVE
A HOUSE IN HEAVEN,
AN ETERNAL BODY MADE FOR US
BY GOD HIMSELF
AND NOT BY HUMAN HANDS.
2 CORINTHIANS 5:1

You Are Eternal

You may have heard the old saying, "All good things come to an end." Sad, huh? But, it isn't true because one important thing never ends. You belong to God, so when your life on this earth ends ... your real life doesn't! It goes on forever in a new body made by God Himself. A body with no pain, no defects ... a perfect body.

That may be hard to imagine, but God has promised. In your new body, you live in His presence, in a home Jesus went to heaven to prepare for you. Such perfection, beauty and joy are beyond human comprehension. Because you are God's child, a member of His family, you will be in His presence and together with loved ones who know Him. There will be no pain, no illness, no separation, no struggles. Only worship, love and celebration. Eternal joy!

Joy is the serious business of heaven.

C. S. Lewis

26

"You" Are Gone

The "original you" died when you came into God's family. That is the "you" that chose sin over righteousness; the "you" who chose unkindness over kindness, selfishness over generosity, and hate over love—the "you" who did not have the Holy Spirit living in your heart.

Now you are a "new you" with the strength, wisdom, discernment, and guidance of the Holy Spirit in you. You can become the person you were meant to be—the person God created you to be. That couldn't happen without God. What's more, you have a teacher who is always with you, helping you grow into the new you—Jesus. That growth comes by spending time getting to know Him on an ever-deepening level by studying His Word and talking with Him and listening to Him. The "new you" will learn and grow and reflect Jesus' love to all.

The steady discipline of intimate friendship
with Jesus results in men becoming like Him.

HARRY EMERSON FOSDICK

27

You Are Held

When you fall away it means you become disconnected from a situation, a person, or a belief system. It can be scary to fall away because it feels like you are freefalling and there is nothing to grab onto to stop your fall.

Remember the day when you put your trust in Jesus and submitted your heart to Him? That one simple choice brought you into God's family. You can now trust that He will hold on to you tightly so that you will not fall away from Him. Sure, you may slip once in a while; you may sin, you may doubt, but God will pull you back. He will hold you close, reminding you of His great love for you. He will celebrate when you accept His help and choose to stay close to Him. You are held by His love for you.

Snuggle in God's arms. When you are hurting. When you feel lonely, left out. Let Him cradle you, comfort you, reassure you of His all-sufficient power and love.

KAY ARTHUR

28

You Are Forgiven

Forgiven. What a beautiful word ... and beautiful experience. Someone forgiving you for a wrong deed or hurtful word is kind and sometimes humbling. But forgiveness from the Creator of everything is overwhelming. God forgives every single thought; every act of selfishness, unkindness, judgment, critical spirit, arrogance ... everything. You are forgiven. Totally forgiven because of Jesus.

Think for a moment about the miracle that when God looks at you He doesn't see your sin. He sees a child whom He loves unconditionally. He sees His child who gratefully accepted Jesus' sacrificial payment for her sin. He sees His child who submitted her sinful, stubborn heart to Jesus and now daily confesses sins and lives to know Him better and live for Him moment by moment because she is forgiven. Do not take God's forgiveness lightly. It is a daily dose of love and grace.

To be a Christian means to forgive the inexcusable,
because God has forgiven the inexcusable in you.
C. S. LEWIS

29

You Are Cared For

What's weighing you down today? Is there a worry that keeps you awake at night? A concern that creeps into your thoughts as you read Scripture or pray? Do you struggle to give these things to God and leave them with Him? That's a hard thing to do because you have to patiently wait on His timing and then you must trust His answer because you trust His heart.

The thing is that God truly cares about any worries that keep you awake at night. He wants to take away whatever struggles intrude in your Bible reading time and prayer time. No concern or struggle is too small for Him to care. Nothing is insignificant because He cares about every aspect of your life. You are truly cared for ... by someone who can do something about the things that worry you! Trust His love. Trust His heart.

God is completely sovereign. God is infinite in wisdom.
God is perfect in love. God in His love always wills what is
best for us. In His wisdom He always knows what is best,
and in His sovereignty He has the power to bring it about.

JERRY BRIDGES

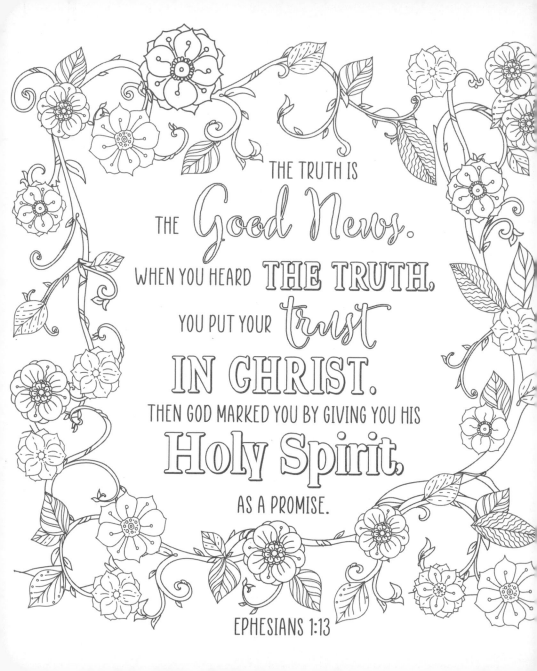

THE TRUTH IS
THE *Good News.*
WHEN YOU HEARD THE TRUTH,
YOU PUT YOUR *trust*
IN CHRIST.
THEN GOD MARKED YOU BY GIVING YOU HIS
Holy Spirit,
AS A PROMISE.

EPHESIANS 1:13

30

You Are Saved

Since the day you accepted Jesus, have you thought about what you are saved from? Your trust in Jesus means you are saved from eternal separation from God. You are promised forever with Him in His heaven, a place of peace, joy, love and worship. You are saved from judgment. You are saved from the condemnation of your sin, which would keep you from God's presence. You are saved from the struggle of living without God's guidance, strength and blessing in your life.

Your salvation gives you the blessed privilege of being indwelt by the Holy Spirit who guides you, gives wisdom and discernment, and even prays for what's on your heart when you can't find the words. "Saved" means a heart that's comforted and strengthened, a peace that is not found anywhere else, and the promise of an amazing forever.

Saving us is the greatest and most concrete demonstration of God's love, the definitive display of His grace throughout time and eternity.

DAVID JEREMIAH

31

You Are Rested

Are you tired (who isn't these days)? Are you completely worn out physically and emotionally? Are you feeling that there's no relief in sight? When you look to the future, is the only bright light you see a train racing toward you? Yes, life can be like that. Situations and people can wear you down, but there is relief ... Jesus.

He loves you so much that He wants to lighten your load, to take those worries off your heart and those struggles out of your mind. Give them to Him. Trust Him to take care of them. Believe that His plan is best. You may need to do this multiple times a day (or night). That's OK, keep praying and give back to Him what your heart has once again snatched away. Give it to Him over and over. Letting go is the hard part, rest is the blessing.

Once I knew what it was to rest upon the rock of God's promises, and it was indeed a precious resting place, but now I rest in His grace. He is teaching me that the bosom of His love is a far sweeter resting place than even the rock of His promises.

HANNAH WHITALL SMITH

32

You Are a Finisher

"Keep on keeping on" is the theme of today's Scripture reading. You do not give up on your relationship with Jesus because you believe with all your heart that it's the most important thing in life. You finish the race you've begun and keep learning how to be like Jesus. You pray and study so you can grow deeper in your faith. Even when you stumble into sin ... or intentionally choose to do or say what you know in your heart is not honoring to God, you ask His help in getting back on your feet and strength to persevere.

The prize you are called to is being in His presence for eternity at the end of the race. But, the journey itself is a prize because of the blessing of knowing His love, trusting His heart, and experiencing His grace. The entire journey is the prize of knowing and loving God.

Perseverance is more than endurance. It is endurance combined with absolute assurance and certainty that what we are looking for is going to happen.

OSWALD CHAMBERS

We are THE AROMA OF Christ TO GOD AMONG THOSE WHO ARE BEING saved AND AMONG THOSE WHO ARE PERISHING

2 CORINTHIANS 2:15

33

You Are a Sweet Aroma

Scents have so much power. Just a whiff of a certain scent can send you back to a pleasant childhood memory. A smell can remind you of a favorite person whom you haven't seen in a long time or won't see again until heaven. Scents can make you very nostalgic, happy or even sad.

God knows that you leave a "scent" wherever you go. That scent comes through attitudes, words and behaviors. The aroma you are called to leave is the aroma of Christ. That would be a positive, kind, encouraging, loving and caring aroma. The way you treat others makes a difference. The words you leave behind make a difference. The attitude you present makes a difference. Those who don't yet know Jesus' love can be drawn to Him by the aroma you leave behind. Your desire to reflect Jesus to all around you leaves a sweet aroma of His love!

Come, Lord, stir us up and call us back. Kindle and seize us.
Be our fire and our sweetness. Let us love. Let us run.

AUGUSTINE OF HIPPO

34

You Are a Child

A baby does nothing to gain the privilege of being chosen for adoption into a family. The prospective parents choose which child to adopt then bring her into their family and love her with all their hearts because she is now their child.

You did nothing to "make" God adopt you into His family. He was waiting to adopt you when you gave your heart to Jesus. As soon as you did that, you were brought into God's family. Now, you enjoy the intimacy of a family relationship with Him. The warmth and acceptance. The support and love. The daily privileges and the promise of eternal inheritance. The security of belonging. You didn't have to earn the right or buy the privilege to be adopted into this beautiful family, it is yours by the blessing of His grace. He loves you to eternity and back. He's your Father.

Always remember that under the New Covenant,
God loves us as much as He loves Jesus for we are in Him.

GLORIA COLEMAN

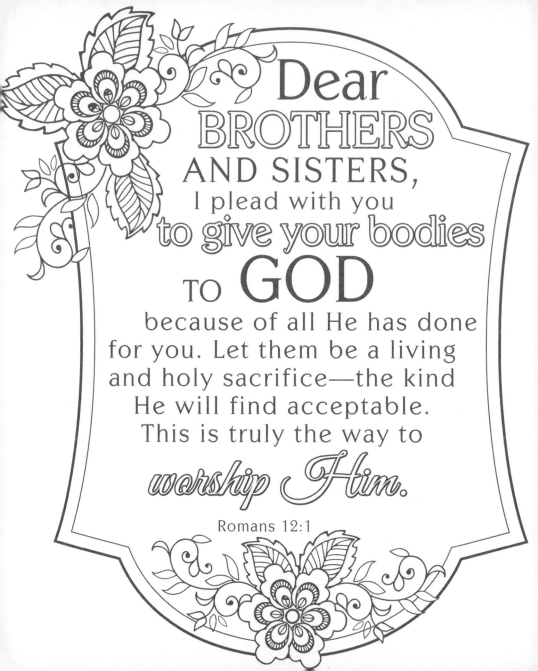

Dear
BROTHERS
AND SISTERS,
I plead with you
to give your bodies
TO GOD
because of all He has done
for you. Let them be a living
and holy sacrifice—the kind
He will find acceptable.
This is truly the way to
worship Him.

Romans 12:1

35

You Are a Sacrifice

When you look at others and think they are so talented and blessed that their service for God must be more useful to Him than you can be, your self-talk goes negative. You may feel God overlooked you when handing out talents. How could you possibly be of any use to Him?

Here's the thing, God made you exactly as He wants you to be so He knows what abilities you have. What He truly wants from you is … you … regardless of what your abilities are. Give Him your whole self. Your time, your energy, your thoughts, your words. Sacrifice all of yourself to Him and He will use you as He planned. That's your worship to Him; your use to Him; your privilege in being a part of God's work. Hold back nothing of what He has given you from His use.

Do all the good you can, by all the means you can,
in all the places you can, at all the times you can,
to all the people you can, as long as ever you can.

JOHN WESLEY

GOD BLESSES

THOSE WHO PATIENTLY
ENDURE TESTING & TEMPTATION.
AFTERWARD THEY WILL RECEIVE THE

CROWN

of life

THAT GOD HAS PROMISED TO THOSE WHO

LOVE HIM.

JAMES 1:12

36

You Are Tested

The reality is that life is hard. Painful situations happen and can last until you begin to wonder if God is paying attention. You beg Him to make the hard things stop. But nothing changes, so then what? You wait. You get up every day, put one foot in front of the other, and trust that God sees what's happening and that He has a plan. You endure.

Hard times aren't a mistake, whether God allows them or brings them Himself, there's purpose in them. When you see God meeting you where you are, providing the strength and endurance to get you through the hard times, you'll trust Him more for the next time troubles come. Trust in one small test and trust grows stronger for a bigger test. You see His love for you and care for what you're facing. You've been tested and found true and you are blessed.

The will of God will not take us where
the grace of God cannot sustain us.
BILLY GRAHAM

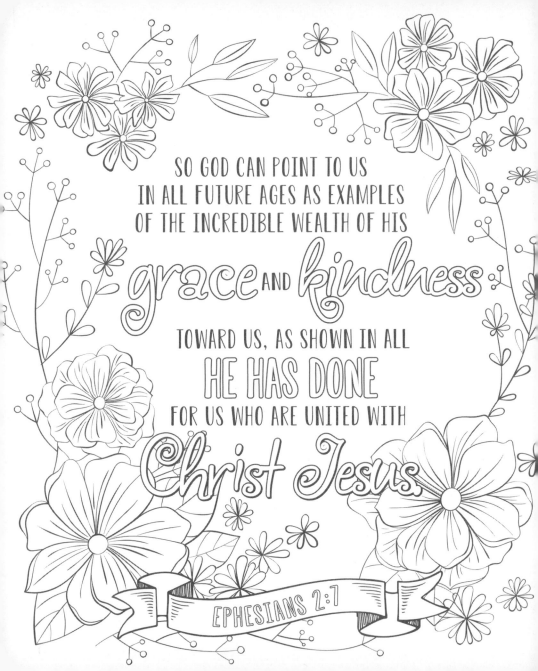

SO GOD CAN POINT TO US
IN ALL FUTURE AGES AS EXAMPLES
OF THE INCREDIBLE WEALTH OF HIS

grace AND *kindness*

TOWARD US, AS SHOWN IN ALL

HE HAS DONE

FOR US WHO ARE UNITED WITH

Christ Jesus

EPHESIANS 2:7

37

You Are an Example

The way you live your life should reflect Jesus to all around you. It should be evident that He is in you and that living for Jesus makes a difference in you. When others say you seem to have supernatural strength in difficult times, give God the credit. If you live out incredible patience, share that it comes from God.

When you are able to show grace to others, be quick to share how His grace is shown to you. Live your faith out loud so that your example of God's blessings and love is heard by all with whom you come in contact. God calls you to be an example in all you say and do. Sometimes actions and behaviors speak much louder than words. Plus, if your behavior doesn't match what you speak about your life in Christ, those words lose their power.

The deeds you do may be the only sermon some people will hear today.

FRANCIS OF ASSISI

38

You Are Friends

Jesus says you are His friend. How amazing is that? There is an intimacy in friendship that goes deeper than coworker or servant. When you are a servant or just work for someone, you are not privileged to know what plans are being made. You simply do what you're told to do. But friends share plans, dreams, hopes, and even fears that others are not privileged to hear.

What a privilege that God's Son, Jesus—your Savior, Creator, the One who makes everything happen, who controls everything—draws you close to Himself and calls you His friend. You no longer worship Him from afar or from a position of servanthood. You're closer than that. Your friendship is a testimony of His great love for you and it's evidence of His grace in providing a way for you to have a relationship with Him.

For me, Jesus is my cleft in the rock. He is my safest friend, my safe, totally loving, accepting big brother.

ANNE LAMOTT

When YOU HAVE Christ, you are complete. HE IS THE HEAD OVER ALL leaders AND POWERS.

COLOSSIANS 2:10

39

You Are Complete

When something is complete it's done; nothing else is necessary to fulfill you or finish you. Christ is all you need. You are like an unfinished sentence or an uncompleted task without Him. Some have spoken of a God-sized hole in your heart that nothing else can fill but Him. He completes who you were made to be. He fills you with His love for Him and for others. He gives you deeper compassion, fuller grace. He meets you where you are and then takes you further ... to where you are more like Jesus than you ever dreamed you could be.

Does being complete in Christ mean that you don't appreciate your family or friends? Of course not, they are a gift from Him who makes you complete because He knows the joy they will bring you. All the blessings in your life are from Him. Everything comes from Him who completes you.

Outside of Christ, I am only a sinner, but in Christ, I am saved.
Outside of Christ, I am empty; in Christ, I am full.
Outside of Christ, I am weak; in Christ, I am strong.
Outside of Christ, I cannot; in Christ, I am more than able.
Outside of Christ, I have been defeated; in Christ, I am already victorious. How meaningful are the words, "in Christ."

WATCHMAN NEE

40

You Are Peaceful

Everyone wants peace and it is attainable … for a moment or two. However, the pace of life with careers, parenting, relationships, and a myriad of responsibilities chips away at peace.

How is peace defined for you? Sitting quietly beside a gentle stream? Relaxing on your patio with a cup of tea? Those can be moments of peace. But in the chaos of life, peace is more. It is an inner knowledge, an assurance, that someone greater than you has everything under control. It is knowing that whatever is going on, Jesus has your back. As your world is falling apart, Jesus is picking up the pieces. When you see no solution to problems, He has a plan.

The peace that Jesus promises is based on your trust that He is who He says He is and He is powerful enough and loving enough to handle anything and everything. Jesus is your peace.

No one can have the peace of God until they are at peace with God.

JACK WELLMAN

You yourselves like living stones are
being built up as a spiritual house, to be a
holy priesthood, to offer spiritual sacrifices
acceptable to God through Jesus Christ.

1 Peter 2:5

41

You Are a Living Stone

Jesus is using you to build His church. Could He do it without you? Sure, but He gives you the privilege of being a living stone in the worldwide structure of faith. Your daily choice to know Jesus, to talk with Him, confess your sins, learn and grow as you read the Bible, to live your faith in front of others makes you a building block in God's plan for the message of His love to be shared with the world.

Interestingly, this verse calls you a living stone, meaning that Christ's church is alive. It's a living, breathing, growing, and changing entity. You, as a building stone, are living, breathing, growing, and changing. Your honest, living worship brings life to the church. Be alive. Be intentional. Be real. Be relevant. Be a living stone that brings energy and passion to God's spiritual house.

We never grow closer to God when we just live life.
It takes deliberate pursuit and attentiveness.

FRANCIS CHAN

WE KNOW THAT NO CHILD OF GOD KEEPS ON SINNING.

THE *Son* OF GOD watches OVER HIM & the devil CANNOT GET NEAR *him.*

1 JOHN 5:18

42

You Are Protected

How beautiful is this? You don't want to keep on sinning. But that's what Satan wants. He wants nothing more than to worm his way close to you so he can trip up your life of faith. He wants to make you doubt your worth to God and God's love for you. He wants you to keep on intentionally making choices that you know are sin.

However, Jesus wants nothing more than to protect you from Satan's efforts. There is a spiritual battle going on all around you, all the time. You are the prize to be won in that battle. Jesus is your shield. He deflects Satan's arrows. He guards you from Satan's sneaky attacks. Jesus is constantly fighting for you and protecting you. All you must do is choose to ignore the thoughts Satan plants in your mind. Choose Jesus' protection and thank Him for always being with you.

Through many dangers, toils and snares
I have already come. 'Tis grace hath brought
me safe thus far and grace will lead me home.

JOHN NEWTON

YOU ARE children OF THE light AND OF THE DAY.

WE ARE NOT OF DARKNESS OR OF NIGHT.

1 THESSALONIANS 5:5

You Are Daylight

Jesus says you are light in this world. Your light is His Spirit in you. The Holy Spirit's light shining through you reveals what's happening in the darkness around you. How? By the love you show by living in the Spirit. It's in sharp contrast to those who live in darkness and with little love and compassion; who have instead settled into self-centeredness and selfishness.

Light reveals sin in the darkness. Without needing to say a word, you can be an example of what it means to live a life of kindness to others, concern for injustices, loving your neighbor, fairness, and honesty. The light of God's Spirit in you shows those stuck in the darkness what life with Jesus looks like. Light is revealing. Light is warm. Light lets you see those around you. Don't fear the darkness. Live in the light.

We aren't called to shine our own lights, we are called to reflect His.

ANONYMOUS

44

You Are Trusting

You obey God because you believe He loves you and has a better plan for your life than you could ever come up with. Love and trust go hand in hand. Can you trust someone you don't love? Can you love someone you don't trust? No, love and trust must go together. When you first met Jesus you loved and trusted Him on a foundational level. The deeper your relationship with Him has grown the more your love and trust has grown.

The key word in this verse is "complete." You must come to God with complete trust. That means no wavering, no doubting, no "I'm going to handle some of life by myself" plans. Trust Him with completely everything because you know that His help is always going to be there for you. You trust because you know He loves you. He takes care of you because He loves you.

Never be afraid to trust an unknown future to a known God.

Corrie Ten Boom

"IF you love me, you will keep my commandments." John 14:15

45

You Are a Commandment-Keeper

Jesus loves you. He is your friend. However, He is also your God and He is a jealous God. He will not share your heart with anyone or anything else. You're either all in with Him or you're not. He has given commandments to be obeyed, not because He wants to keep you under His thumb but because He knows that obeying His commandments and living as He teaches in Scripture is for your own good.

Obeying Him makes life better for you and those around you. Obeying Him shows that you respect and honor Him. Declaring your love for Him but ignoring His commandments is a flat-out lie. Disobedience makes your words of obedience worthless. Jesus trusts that when you accept Him as Savior, you will make every effort to obey His commands. Will you stumble sometimes? Sure, but His forgiveness is given to a repentant heart.

Wicked men obey from fear; good men from love.
St. Augustine

God is able to make all grace abound to you, so that having all sufficiency in all things at all times, you may abound in every good work.

2 Corinthians 9:8

46

You Have All You Need

You have everything you need to be all God planned for you to be! Everything is under God's control so He can empower you, gift you and bless you with what you need. Do you have trouble loving someone? Tell God. He will give you the love you need. Do you struggle with a certain temptation over and over?

Ask God for strength to fight it off. Has God asked you to do something that's out of your comfort zone? He will give you the strength, creativity, courage, and whatever else you need to do the work. By His grace, He gives you all you need to do what He wants you to do. Remember, too, that you are not saved just for your own wellbeing but so you can spread the message of God's love to others. Use the blessings He gives you and do the good work He calls you to do.

Ministering Christ to others so that Jesus might be reproduced and grow in people is the highest service to both God and man.

HENRY HON

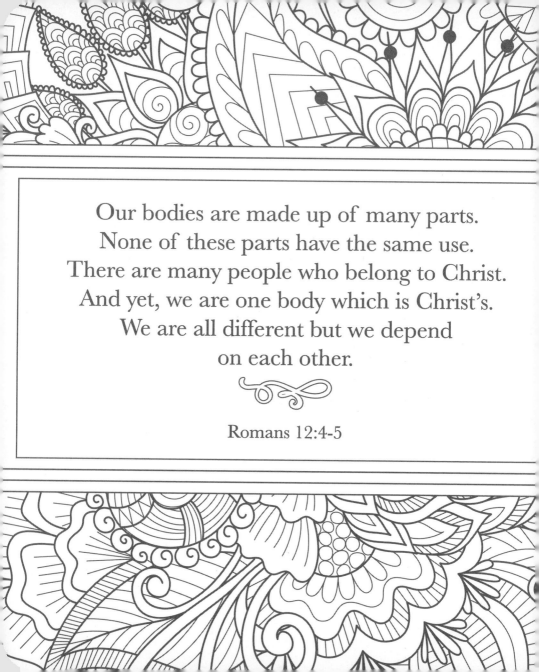

Our bodies are made up of many parts.
None of these parts have the same use.
There are many people who belong to Christ.
And yet, we are one body which is Christ's.
We are all different but we depend
on each other.

Romans 12:4-5

47

You Are Part of the Body

God sees the big picture of life. He put you exactly where you are because that particular local body of believers needs the uniqueness you bring to them. You don't have to be all things to all people. You only need to be the best you that you can be.

God, in His wisdom, made you a part of a group of believers who work together, complementing each other in your service to God. Don't get caught up in jealousy that you can't do what another person does, or think that what you do isn't important. Just like your physical body, every part of God's body is needed to make a healthy, functioning body. Commit to being a great team player by doing whatever work, big or small, God gives you to do. Pray for your partners. Support them and celebrate the honor of doing God's work together.

We are the body of Christ, many members,
many differences ... and you play an important part.
COLLEEN SWINDOLL

48

You Are the Reason

Why did God plan for Jesus to come to earth and die a sacrificial death? Why did He allow His precious, beloved Son to leave the glory of heaven and face the torment He did on earth? Why was Jesus willing to do it? He had all the glories of heaven. He had angels serving Him. He was with His Father.

Jesus had absolutely everything … except for one thing … He didn't have you. Jesus and His Father agreed that He should come to earth to teach and heal and love. He willingly left the glory of heaven, suffered the torment and hatred of mankind, experienced a horrible crucifixion and separation from His Father as He paid the debt for your sin. Why? Because He loves you and wanted to make a way for you to have a personal relationship with His Father.

God proved His love on the cross. When Christ hung, and bled, and died, it was God saying to the world, "I love you."

BILLY GRAHAM

49

You Are the Spirit's

After His resurrection, Jesus went back to heaven but before He left He promised to send the Holy Spirit to His followers. The Spirit lives in your heart and is God's presence with you every moment. The Spirit is your helper, guiding you into wise decisions. He fills you with the fruit of what it means to live for Jesus—love, joy, peace, patience, kindness, goodness, faithfulness, gentleness and self-control.

He challenges you to be obedient to God's commandments. When you are troubled and simply can't find the words to pray, the Spirit prays for you. He guards and guarantees your salvation. The Spirit also gives you what you need to do the work God gives you to do. He helps you understand God. The Spirit is alive within you helping you grow and learn how to serve God.

The Spirit-filled life is not a special, deluxe edition of Christianity.
It is part and parcel of the total plan of God for His people.

A. W. TOZER

BEFORE daybreak the next *morning,* *Jesus* got up and went out to an isolated *place* to pray.

MARK 1:35

50

You Follow Jesus' Example

How important is prayer to you? No doubt you would say prayer matters, but think honestly about it. Does your life get so busy that prayer gets relegated to times when you have a crisis? Are you likely to pour out your heart to the Lord? Is prayer important enough that you absolutely must start your day with it? It was that important to Jesus. He went out by Himself, before the sun came up, just to pray. You read in Scripture several times about Jesus going off by Himself to pray. As busy as He was, and though He was constantly surrounded by people, it was a priority for Jesus to go off by Himself and talk to His Father.

Because you follow Jesus' example, prayer is a priority for you, too. Telling God what's on your heart and thanking Him for all He does for you. These are priorities.

Fervent prayers produce phenomenal results.

WOODROW KROLL

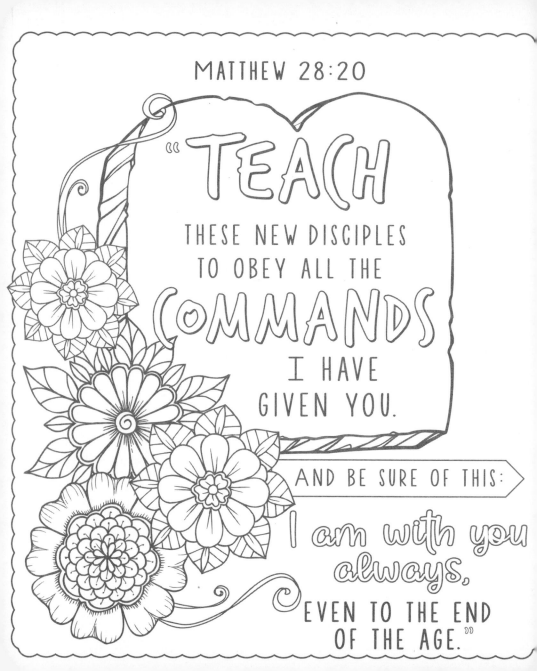

51

You Are a Teacher

Your life is bigger than just your life. Jesus instructs you to look beyond yourself to help others know Him better. No matter how long you have been a believer, it's likely that you have learned things another person may not have learned yet. Share what you know and teach others how to know God on a deeper level, how to serve Him more humbly, how to live more sacrificially and how to obey Him more readily.

Challenge others to study Scripture and learn what it means to obey His commands. Take seriously the work of sharing what you have learned. Don't be intimidated by the responsibility. Don't feel that you are doing it alone. You aren't—Jesus promised to always be with you. Through the guidance and wisdom of His Holy Spirit, you will have the right words to say at the right time.

Expect great things from God. Attempt great things for God.

WILLIAM CAREY

52

You Have the Mind of Christ

You may not understand what God is doing, but you do know that He's working out His plan in the world and you trust that whatever He's doing is good. After all, you wouldn't want to know everything He knows. If you did, you'd be all He is ... then why worship and trust Him? He reveals things to you as you need to know them and for everything else, you trust.

A person who doesn't know Christ cannot begin to understand obeying His commands, following His guidance, or trusting His heart. Things of God seem like silliness to them. But you have the Spirit who guides you. He helps you understand ways to care for others and lift others up. He guides you in sharing His love with others and ways to disciple others in spiritual growth. The blessing of knowing Christ is that you have His Spirit who helps you understand and know His mind.

Not only do we not know God except through Jesus Christ;
we do not even know ourselves except through Jesus Christ.

BLAISE PASCAL

WE ALSO

rejoice

IN GOD

THROUGH OUR LORD JESUS CHRIST,
THROUGH WHOM WE HAVE NOW
RECEIVED RECONCILIATION.

ROMANS 5:11

You Are Reconciled

How wonderful would it be if someone came along and paid off every debt you owe? What if this was done with no strings attached—purely as a gift? What if it cost that person a lot to pay your debt? Still, you would get a notice that your account is paid in full. You have no further obligation.

The biggest debt you have ever (or will ever) owe has been settled, paid in full. Jesus has reconciled (settled) the debt for your sin. It cost Him a lot—suffering and finally death—to settle your debt. There's no way you could ever have paid that debt for yourself, so be thankful, be grateful. Don't be lackadaisical in your gratitude. Celebrate! Rejoice! However rejoicing looks for you—dance, sing, shout, laugh, share. Give your rejoicing your all—to the magnitude of the hugeness of this gift!

Genuine thankfulness is an act of the heart's
affections, not an act of the lips' muscles.

JOHN PIPER

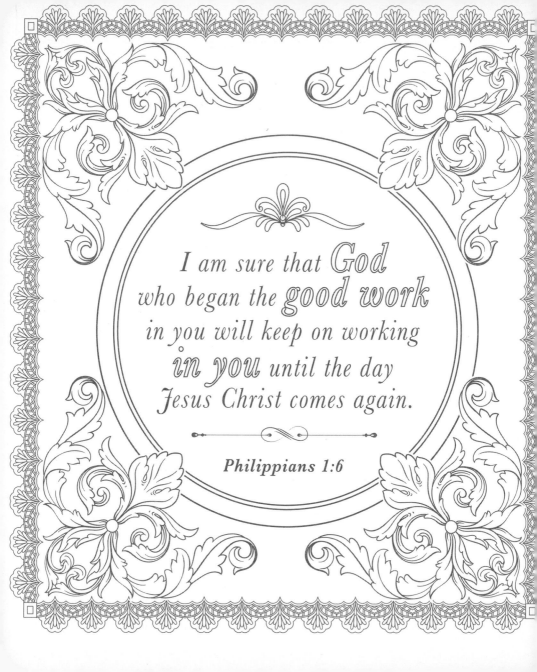

I am sure that *God*
who began the *good work*
in you will keep on working
in you until the day
Jesus Christ comes again.

Philippians 1:6

54

You Are a Work in Progress

Okay, so you're not perfect. Guess what? God doesn't expect you to be. You are a work in progress. God knows what you can be ... what you will be someday and He's watching your progress. That takes the pressure off, doesn't it? The wonderful thing is that while He sees today's failures and shortcomings, He also sees your heart's desire to do better ... to be better.

The moment you first accepted Christ as Savior He began working in your heart, teaching you about Himself, encouraging you to love and trust Him, and showing you how to love your neighbor as yourself. Even on the days when you don't feel as though you're making progress, God sees that you are. So don't be hard on yourself when you fail. Look at all you've learned so far and celebrate as Christ continues teaching you!

When I release my weaknesses and blind spots to God,
He uses them to help me grow up spiritually.

CRYSTAL McDOWELL

WE ARE *pressed* ON EVERY SIDE BY TROUBLES, BUT WE ARE NOT CRUSHED. WE ARE *perplexed*, BUT NOT DRIVEN TO DESPAIR.

2 CORINTHIANS 4:8

55

You Cannot Be Defeated

Jesus did not promise that your life would be problem-free once you accepted Him as Savior. In fact, He promised the opposite. Life does get complicated in this messy world. Relationships, financial issues, health problems, natural disasters—the opportunities for difficulties are endless. Do not expect to avoid problems. What Jesus did promise is that you will not … cannot be defeated by anything or anyone in this world because you are His.

Jesus is more powerful than anything life can throw at you and His strength, power, grace, wisdom, and love will see you through any difficulty. You are His. When life gets tough, don't give up. Turn to Him when you're scared, tired, confused, and even when you feel hopeless. Lean on Him. Trust Him. The power that created the world, parted the Red Sea, and raised Jesus back to life is yours because you are His!

What gives me the most hope every day is God's grace; knowing that His grace is going to give me the strength for whatever I face, knowing that nothing is a surprise to God.
RICK WARREN

PUT ON THE

new self,

created AFTER THE

LIKENESS

OF

God IN TRUE

RIGHTEOUSNESS

AND *holiness.*

EPHESIANS 4:24

56

You Are a New Person

You are a new you! Jesus has peeled off your original sinful self. He made you a new person and gave you a new heart, filled with the desire to be like God. A new self that wants to submit to God and follow His will. A new self that sees His power and strength; respects His holiness and honors Him the way He deserves. A new self that cares deeply for others and explores ways to share God's love with them. A new self that searches for ways to lift others above yourself and desires to serve others. A new self that reflects your righteous God.

Now, is that behavior and attitude always present? Probably not, but it is the desire of your new self. Putting on this new self is a daily choice of submission to God and allowing His Spirit to work in your new heart.

Let God have your life; He can do more with it than you can.
DWIGHT L. MOODY

Whoever HAS THE Son has life;

whoever does not have
God's Son does not have life.

1 JOHN 5:12

57

You Have Life

Is this verse speaking only of the promise of life in heaven with God once you leave life on this earth? That's a great promise for sure, but does this verse have any other meaning?

When you accepted Jesus as Savior, the Holy Spirit came to live in your heart, giving your life greater meaning by a deep connection to God. His presence makes your life richer. Your relationship with Him gives you purpose and direction. Sure, your life before Jesus may have been good because you enjoyed good friendships and a loving family. Even those relationships can now be deeper and richer with the shared experience of God's love in your lives.

Life in the Son is better because of the focus and direction and love He gives you now. It will be better in the future because you will have life forever, with Him. Life with God is a double blessing!

Take care of your life and the Lord will take care of your death.
GEORGE WHITEFIELD

58

You Have Trusted

The act of putting your trust in Jesus changes everything for you. However, it's not always so simple, is it? Trust is an interesting emotion. It's not possible to "sort of" trust. You either trust or you don't. If you're holding any area of your life back from God ... well ... you're not trusting, are you?

Trusting the Lord completely means you fully believe His plan is always for your best. You believe His love for you and those you love is honest, sincere, and complete. You hold nothing and no one back because whatever He brings or allows in your life, you know it will serve to grow your faith in Him. Deeper trust makes you a more devoted child of God and that means His power is even more present in your life. More trust brings more power.

I will trust Him. Whatever, wherever I am, I can never be thrown away. If I am in sickness, my sickness may serve Him; in perplexity, my perplexity may serve Him; if I am in sorrow, my sorrow may serve Him. My sickness or perplexity or sorrow may be necessary causes of some great end, which is quite beyond us. He does nothing in vain.

JOHN HENRY NEWMAN

EACH OF YOU SHOULD CONTINUE TO live IN WHATEVER SITUATION THE LORD HAS PLACED YOU, & REMAIN AS YOU WERE WHEN GOD FIRST CALLED you. THIS IS MY RULE FOR ALL THE CHURCHES.

1 CORINTHIANS 7:17

59

You Are Where You Should Be

"You'll never have the life you want until you want the life you have."
Does this quote by Mallory Redmond make sense to you or does it
make you feel that you must settle for less than what you hoped?
Think about that statement in the context of 1 Corinthians 7:17.
God has put you where He wants you to be so that your gifts and
talents can complement those in your community.

Working together you can accomplish His plan for your part
of the world. Living in peace, working hard, following His will,
encouraging those around you, and simply doing the work He has
placed you there to do is your obedience to Him. And obedience
grows faith and blessings. Being content where God has placed
you makes the work you do for God all the more productive
and the experience of working with others more pleasant. Your
contentment gives you the life you want.

Next to faith this is the highest art—to be content
in the calling in which God has placed you.
MARTIN LUTHER

I AM CONVINCED THAT NOTHING CAN EVER *separate* US FROM GOD'S *love.*

ROMANS 8:38

Neither death nor life, neither angels nor demons, neither our fears for today nor our worries about tomorrow—not even the powers of hell can separate us from GOD'S LOVE.

60

You Are Secure

God loves you, no matter what. How sweet is that? He is going nowhere and nothing life throws at you has the power to make His love stop. Not even your death, because leaving this life moves you right into His precious heaven. There is no better place to be. Nothing that Satan attacks you with can defeat God's love. God is stronger and more powerful than the evil one so hold on tight to God! Even more wonderful is that you cannot defeat God's love for you.

Your worries, your fears, your self-doubts … none of those are greater than God's love. Think about it—He has loved you through your failures, your doubts, your disappointments, and your joys and successes. You can rest in the secure knowledge that you are locked in by a love so deep, so great and strong that nothing can rip you away from it.

Though our feelings come and go, God's love for us does not.

C. S. LEWIS

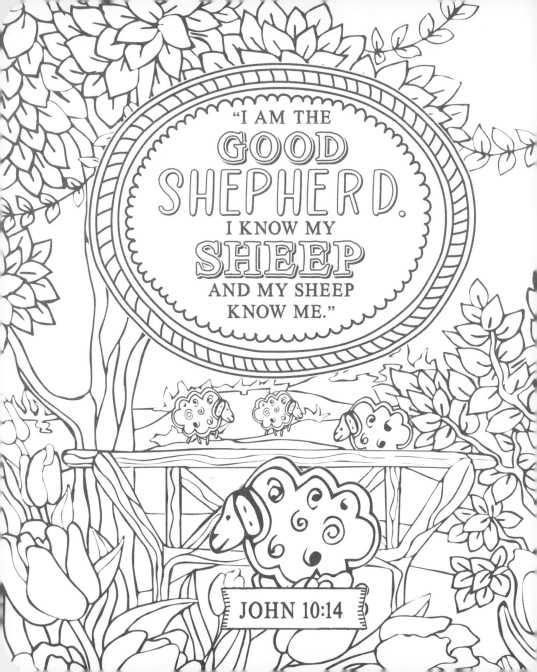

61

You Have a Shepherd

Here's good news—you don't have to figure life out by yourself. Sometimes life gets a bit muddled. Choices can seem foggy and you may not know which direction to go. But, the Good Shepherd is ready to guide you. He knows you. He knows your abilities and talents. He knows your shortcomings. He knows your desires, hopes, and dreams. He has a plan for your life, a plan that will give you usefulness and purpose in your days. He knows what you need and where you need to go. He is your Shepherd and will guide your life.

Stay close to Jesus by reading His Word. Be still and let Him speak to you. Stay so close that you recognize His voice over the chaos of other voices shouting for your attention. The more time you spend with Him the better you will be able to recognize His voice.

The willingness to obey every word from
God is critical to hearing God speak.
Henry T. Blackaby

We are God's masterpiece. He has created us anew in Christ Jesus, so we can do the good things He planned for us long ago.

Ephesians 2:10

62

You Are God's Masterpiece

A masterpiece is an artist's best work. It's a work that other people study and admire. You are God's masterpiece! Think about all God created—the oceans, sky, stars, sun, and moon. He made grand canyons, mountains, and rainforests. He made so many amazing things ... but you are His best work.

When you accepted Jesus as Savior, the old you disappeared. That's the sinful you who didn't care about knowing or obeying God. But the new you is made in the image of Jesus. The new you is loving and devoted to knowing and obeying God. Maybe you don't always feel like a masterpiece. That's OK. God sees that your heart is focused on Jesus. He knows, even on days you stumble, that you long to bring honor to Him and share Jesus' love by how you live your life.

God is the Master Artist. Never forget that you are His masterpiece.

ANONYMOUS

63

You Are Strong

Reading through the Bible you see story after story of God's incredible strength. Story after story of how He parted seas, sent floods, stopped the sun from moving, sent fire from heaven to burn offerings, made a city's walls fall down, healed the sick, raised the dead—including His Son, Jesus Christ. Scripture is filled with amazing stories of strength greater than any other power or being.

From the moment you accepted Jesus as Savior, that incredible strength became available to you. Why? Because God has a plan for your life. He has work for you to do and you will need His strength to do it. There will be times of discouragement, times of failure, times of persecution and it is His strength that will get you through. There is nothing ... absolutely nothing that can defeat you when you call on God for help. His strength is the greatest.

When God wants to move a mountain, He does not take a bar of iron, but He takes a little worm. The fact is, we have too much strength. We are not weak enough. It is not our strength that we want. One drop of God's strength is worth more than all the world.

DWIGHT L. MOODY

64

You Are an Overcomer

Jesus promises peace. He also promises trouble. The reality is that you won't understand peace unless you have also experienced trouble. Accepting Jesus doesn't give you a shield against problems. You'll still have hard times, difficult relationships, and failures. Those are all part of being alive in this fallen world.

Peace comes when you trust Jesus to guide you in resolving problems or making it through them in a way that honors Him. There may be times when you can see no resolution and have little hope for peace. That's when your faith kicks into high gear because of your trust in Jesus. He has overcome the world and His strength is greater than any problems you face or any difficult people you deal with. He has overcome the world and with His strength, you can overcome anything facing you, too!

Faith in God has not saved people from hardships
and trials, but it has enabled them to bear tribulations
courageously and to emerge victoriously.

LEE ROBERSON

2 Corinthians 12:10

I receive joy
when I am weak.
I receive joy when people
talk against me
and make it hard for me
and try to hurt me
and make trouble for me.
I receive joy
when all these things
come to me because
of Christ.

For when I am weak,
then I am strong.

65

You Are Joy-Filled

Is it difficult to think about being joyful when you're going through hard times? You may just be putting one foot in front of the other and getting through day by day. If that's the case, do these words just make you feel guilty? What do they mean? Of course, you realize that happiness and joy are not the same.

Happiness is great. It usually comes because of good news or a certain situation. It feels good, of course ... but it doesn't last. It's a surface emotion. Joy is not dependent on emotions. It's not dependent on situations or kind words or good news. Joy comes from deep within and is present regardless of your circumstances. Joy comes from knowing that whatever life brings you, Jesus is in control. His strength and grace walk with you through every situation. You trust Him to bring His good from all things.

The Bible teaches that true joy is formed
in the midst of the difficult seasons of life.

Francis Chan

THE
Holy Spirit

PRODUCES THIS KIND OF
FRUIT IN OUR LIVES:

{ LOVE, JOY, PEACE, PATIENCE,
KINDNESS, GOODNESS,
FAITHFULNESS, GENTLENESS,
AND SELF-CONTROL. }

THERE IS NO LAW AGAINST
THESE THINGS!

GALATIANS 5:22-23

66

You Are Fruitful

A Christ-follower should look different than those who do not belong to Jesus. This fruit that the Holy Spirit produces in you should make you stand out from the crowd. Your kindness and gentleness should be apparent to all who come into contact with you. Does this fruit mean that those who do not know Jesus are never kind, patient, gentle, etc.? Of course not.

There are kind people everywhere. It means that these Spirit-induced fruit characteristics are more consistent in your life and especially toward those to whom it is not easy or palatable to show kindness. These days social media makes sarcasm, cruelty, and being judgmental so easy, but the Spirit helps you resist. Self-control rules. Look different because you are different. Be mindful that every word, attitude and deed is a reflection on God and is a statement of your attitude toward Him.

The fruit of the Spirit is not push, drive, climb, grasp and trample. Life is more than a climb to the top of the heap.

RICHARD J. FOSTER

EPHESIANS 2:8-9

By grace you have been saved through faith.

AND THIS IS NOT YOUR OWN DOING; IT IS THE GIFT OF GOD, NOT A RESULT OF WORKS, SO THAT NO ONE MAY BOAST.

67

You Received Grace

You are saved, not because of anything you did. There was nothing at all you could do. You couldn't buy salvation. You couldn't bargain for it. You didn't deserve it. Salvation is completely a gift from God because of His incredible grace. You have the blessing of being saved from the prison of sin and being sentenced to eternity separated from God. You are saved to the blessing of His presence in your daily life, giving guidance, purpose and direction to your days and constantly teaching you how to live for Him and be a blessing to those around you.

The beautiful thing about this salvation is again, that you did nothing to bring it about—it's all from God. There's no reason to feel you're more deserving or more "saveable" than anyone else. So approach your salvation with humility and gratitude and willingly share your faith with others.

Saving us is the greatest and most concrete demonstration of God's love, the definitive display of His grace throughout time and eternity.

DAVID JEREMIAH

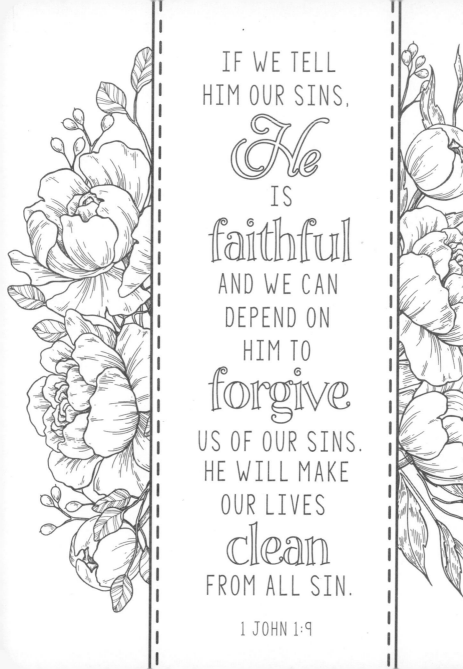

IF WE TELL
HIM OUR SINS,
He
IS
faithful
AND WE CAN
DEPEND ON
HIM TO
forgive
US OF OUR SINS.
HE WILL MAKE
OUR LIVES
clean
FROM ALL SIN.

1 JOHN 1:9

68

You Confess

The bottom line is that your sins are forgiven. Jesus died to pay the price for them. However, His death did not relieve you of the responsibility of owning your shortcomings. You've heard the expression that confession is good for the soul. While it's true that Jesus already knows your sins, it's good for you to know them, too. Take some time each day to ask Him to help you know what your shortcomings and failures have been. You probably know some but maybe not all.

Be still and listen. If you're truly willing to listen, the Spirit will speak into your heart and reveal your sins. It's not easy to hear that you've failed but really hearing can help you learn and grow stronger in your obedience to God. You can trust His forgiveness and that He will wipe your sins away. Your confession cleanses your mind and your heart.

It's Satan's delight to tell me that once he's got me, he will keep me. But at that moment I can go back to God. And I know that if I confess my sins, God is faithful and just to forgive me.

ALAN REDPATH

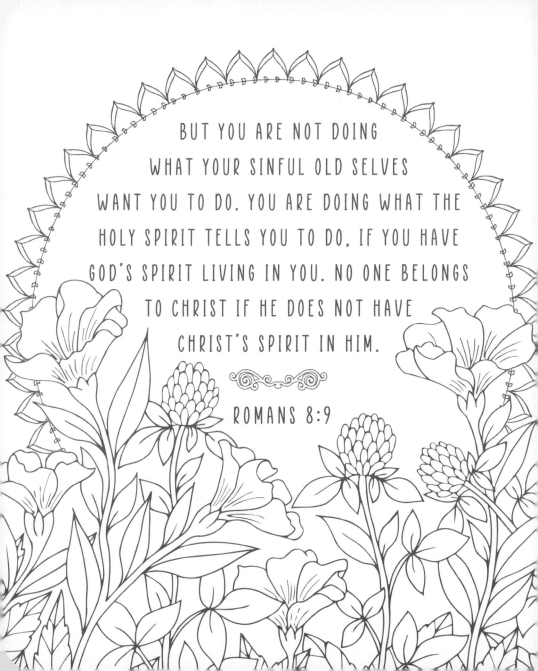

BUT YOU ARE NOT DOING
WHAT YOUR SINFUL OLD SELVES
WANT YOU TO DO. YOU ARE DOING WHAT THE
HOLY SPIRIT TELLS YOU TO DO, IF YOU HAVE
GOD'S SPIRIT LIVING IN YOU. NO ONE BELONGS
TO CHRIST IF HE DOES NOT HAVE
CHRIST'S SPIRIT IN HIM.

ROMANS 8:9

69

You Are Changed

You had a heart rehab when you accepted Jesus. Your original, sinful heart was cleaned up then the Holy Spirit moved in. So, you're changed. The instinctive behaviors you acted on before the rehab are now challenged by the presence of the Holy Spirit.

When you start to act in the old way He says, "Hold on. That behavior won't honor God. It won't model what God's love looks like." See? He convicts you of your old behavior and reminds you to show by your life that Jesus is your Lord. Now, don't beat yourself up if you fail to listen to Him once in a while. You're human. It happens. But learn to pay attention to Him. Those who try to act as though they belong to Jesus without actually having the Spirit will fail because eventually, the old behavior pops out. Not with you though … you are changed!

The indwelling Spirit shall teach him what is of God and
what is not. This is why sometimes we can conjure up
no logical reason for opposing a certain teaching,
yet in the very depth of our being arises a resistance.

WATCHMAN NEE

70

You Are Purchased

Perhaps you've heard the phrase "Freedom isn't free." It usually refers to the price men and women of the military pay for your country's freedom. It can also refer to your freedom from sin. Your freedom didn't cost you anything but it did cost Jesus. Before Jesus, people "bought" their forgiveness or freedom from sin by offering a blood sacrifice to God. It had to happen because God's complete purity could not be stained by the filth of sin. So, people could only get close to Him by offering a sacrifice to cover the cost of their sin.

Jesus changed that. He left heaven to come to earth as a man, be arrested, tortured, crucified and separated from God as He took on the burden of your sin. He paid the price. He bought your freedom. He made it possible for you to have an intimate, personal relationship with God.

We could not become like God, so God became like us.
God showed us how to heal instead of kill, how to mend instead
of destroy, how to love instead of hate, how to live instead
of long for more. When we nailed God to a tree, God forgave.
And when we buried God in the ground, God got up.

Rachel Held Evans

MY OLD SELF HAS BEEN CRUCIFIED WITH CHRIST. IT IS NO LONGER I WHO LIVE, BUT CHRIST LIVES IN ME. SO I LIVE IN THIS EARTHLY BODY BY TRUSTING IN THE SON OF GOD, WHO LOVED ME AND GAVE HIMSELF FOR ME.

Galatians 2:20

71

You Are on a Journey

Christ is doing major work in you and you probably don't always make it easy. He's cutting away the old you which was self-centered and thought about every situation as to how it affected you. He's opening your heart to new ideas, to loving people who are different. He's growing compassion in you for those who are hurting in any way. He's trying to help you learn that serving Him is the only way to a truly fulfilled life.

Of course you want to learn those lessons but the journey isn't always easy. Sometimes your old self fights back. Sometimes Satan squirms his way in to make you resistant. Don't give up. God doesn't give up on you. This process of submitting to Christ living in you is a journey and it won't be perfected until you step into heaven. Keep your feet on the path and your heart in the process.

Whatever God is urging you to clear away cannot begin to be compared to what He ultimately wants to bring you.

BETH MOORE

THE
truth
IS THE
GOOD NEWS.

When you heard the truth,
you put your trust in Christ.
Then God marked you by
giving you His Holy Spirit
as a promise.

Ephesians 1:13

72

You Know the Truth

These days there are many, many voices shouting out what they claim to be truth. With so many voices coming at you, there's a danger that real truth gets lost or even watered down in your efforts to be kind and accepting. But, with the Holy Spirit guiding your thoughts and giving discernment and wisdom, you will know what real truth is. Make time to hear Him. Pay attention to how He guides your thoughts and those convictions and impulses in your heart.

A real truth is the good news that Jesus died for your sins and God raised Him back to life. God loves you more than you can possibly comprehend which is why He sent the Holy Spirit to help you. You know the truth. Hold on to it and don't let the louder voices overpower the quiet strength of real truth—the Good News.

Where I found truth, there found I my God, who is truth itself.

St. Augustine

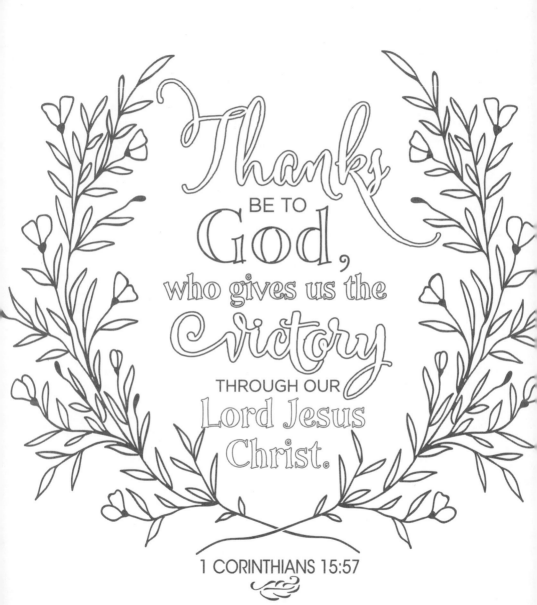

Thanks BE TO God, who gives us the victory THROUGH OUR Lord Jesus Christ.

1 CORINTHIANS 15:57

73

You Are Victorious!

Are you wondering where your victory is hiding? Maybe it seems your problems are piling one on top of the other and your support system feels pretty wobbly. So what's happening? Where is this victory that you're supposed to be thanking God for?

There can't be a victory unless there is a battle. So when problems, struggles and crises are constant in your life, just know that you are definitely in a battle. And, if the disappearance of some of your support system adds to the difficulties, realize that even if everything and everyone in your life disappeared, you still have God and God is all you need. Your victory comes through the support and strength of Jesus Christ. While friends and loved ones are a special gift to you from God, they cannot and should not replace Jesus Himself. Lean on Him and Him only. Your victory comes only through Jesus.

God will sometimes allow things to get bad enough
that we will be forced to look up. Victory always begins
with a cry for help. When we come to the end of ourselves
and cry out for help, amazing things happen.

BETH MOORE

74

You Are Paying Attention

"Keep your head in the game" is a challenge given to athletes in the midst of a game. It's a challenge to pay attention to your opponents, notice what's going on with your own team, and react in a way that gives you opportunities for success. That's essentially what this verse in 1 Peter is saying.

Keep your head in what's going on. Don't get lazy. Pay attention to the sneaky ways Satan tries to pull your focus away from the Lord. Satan is a jealous being who will do anything he can to turn you away from serving God. He will try to make you doubt God's good work and love. Pay attention so you know when those things are happening. Call on Jesus to give you strength to fight off those attacks. He can't beat you because the power of God is fighting for you!

Satan rocks the cradle when we sleep at our devotions.

JOSEPH HALL

Have your roots planted
deep in Christ. Grow in Him.
Get your strength from Him.
Let Him make you strong in the faith as you
have been taught. Your life should be
full of thanks to Him.

Colossians 2:7

75

You Are Fed

Food and water are basic necessities for every living thing. Plants get their food and water through their roots that push through the soil looking for nutrition. You need food and water, too, of course. So you eat and drink to keep your body healthy and strong. But how do you feed your spirit? Remember that whatever you put in your mind and heart determines their health. You draw your spirit's nutrition from Christ Himself by planting your roots in Him as this verse instructs.

You must be intentional in reading the Bible so you learn more about Him and His love and care for you. It's important to talk with Him, tell Him what's on your mind and heart, and then to be still so you can listen for His guidance. Hold tightly to Him so that your strength comes from Him and enables you to resist anything that tries to pull you away from Him.

As many have learned and later taught, you don't realize
Jesus is all you need until Jesus is all you have.

TIM KELLER

1 Peter 3:3-4

Don't be concerned about the outward *beauty* of fancy hairstyles, expensive jewelry, or beautiful clothes You should *clothe yourselves* instead with the *beauty* that comes from within, the unfading beauty of a gentle and quiet spirit, which is so precious to *God.*

76

You Are Beautiful

Media, peers and even you put so much importance on appearance, shouting that you should be thin, pretty and stylish. It's exhausting and it isn't where you should be putting your focus or energy. Sure, it's good to look nice but real beauty is not appearance.

There's a saying, "You can't judge a book by its cover." That's because the good stuff is inside. The beauty that matters, that defines you as a child of God, is the inside beauty of kindness, gentleness, self-control—the fruit of the Spirit. Beauty that's evident in the way you treat others, such as patience with a store clerk, kindness to a neighbor, gentleness with a family member, smiling at a stranger, sharing the life and love of God with all around you. That's true beauty.

In all ranks of life the human heart yearns for the beautiful; and the beautiful things that God makes are His gift to all alike.

HARRIET BEECHER STOWE

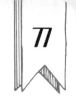

77

You Love Others

In a world where "ME" is increasingly the most important, the sacrifice of Jesus' life is even more incredible. A characteristic of a Jesus-follower is to be other-focused. Paying attention to how your choices and actions impact others. When Jesus walked on this earth, He often put Himself in harm's way by teaching in towns where people wanted to hurt Him. His willingness to come to earth and pay the price for our sins was in itself a sacrificial act beyond compare.

As your life reflects to others who Jesus is, live sacrificially for them. Instead of pushing others down to lift yourself up, do the opposite. Instead of considering how situations affect you, think about the ramifications for others. Jesus said the second greatest commandment is to love your neighbor as yourself. Doing that may not always be easy, but it's living and loving sacrificially.

Intense love does not measure, it just gives.

MOTHER TERESA

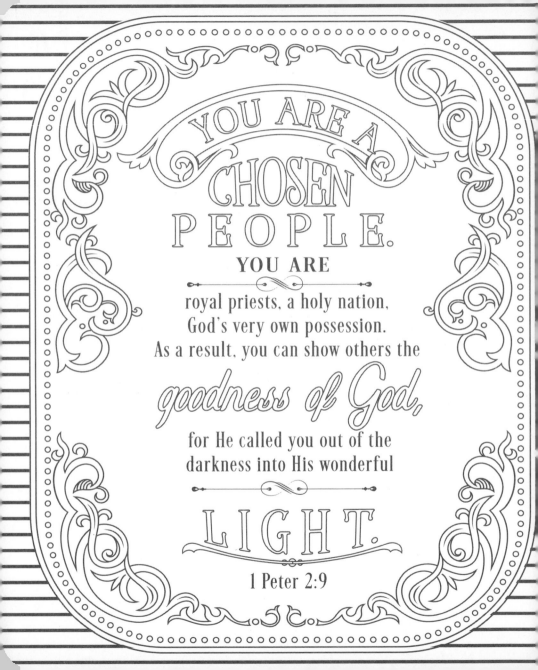

YOU ARE A CHOSEN PEOPLE.

YOU ARE

royal priests, a holy nation,
God's very own possession.
As a result, you can show others the

goodness of God,

for He called you out of the
darkness into His wonderful

LIGHT.

1 Peter 2:9

78

You Belong

Have you ever auditioned for a play or to be a part of a special choir? It's something you really want. It's stressful. You prepare. You fight your nerves. You audition but … you aren't chosen. It hurts. Your mind says that it's OK because you'll be chosen next time but your heart still hurts. You feel unwanted. You don't belong to the group or production that you really wanted to be a part of.

Here's a new reality … God wants you. He looked over all the people on this planet and He chose you. You belong to Him and nothing can change that. It doesn't matter whether you can sing, preach, write, organize or anything else that other people can do. God chose you and has uniquely gifted you to do the work He has for you. You belong.

God is busy making you someone no one else has ever been.

BETH MOORE

By this we
know that we have
come to know Him,
if we keep His
commandments.

1 John 2:3

79

You Obey

A person can claim to know Jesus. She can say all the right words and even quote Bible verses. She may be a good person, but still not be a Christian. Saying the right words and even doing nice things but not obeying Jesus' commands shows what is truly in a person's heart.

Obeying God is not always easy. It's not meant to be. Matthew 7:14 states that the road to heaven is narrow. You must be intentional to stay on it and that won't happen by accident. Choose to know God's commands. Choose to let them settle in you so that they are infused into your heart. Then His Holy Spirit can bring them to mind when you need to be reminded. Your actions will show that His commands mean something to you. Your actions will show that you belong to Him.

When it comes to God's commands,
the issue is not clarity; it is commitment.
WOODROW KROLL

1 JOHN 5:5

WHO IS IT THAT
OVERCOMES THE WORLD EXCEPT THE ONE WHO
BELIEVES THAT JESUS IS THE SON OF GOD?

80

You Have Power

Some groups of people think they have ultimate power in this world. Politicians run our countries, states or provinces, and our towns. The wealthy have influence over almost everything. Sometimes they step on others to climb the ladder of success. Sometimes they oppress others for their own profit. So many people are looking out only for Number One and feeling they have the upper hand in this world. But … they don't. They do not have power over Jesus. The day will come when they answer for their actions.

Your identity in Christ means that you do have power. You belong to the One who has overcome the world. Your yearning to know Him, obey Him, and share His love with others puts you in good standing with Him. Live as one who has the power to show love, compassion, and generosity to all. Use your power for good.

If you look up into His face and say, "Yes, Lord, whatever it costs,"
at that moment He will flood your life with His presence and power.

Alan Redpath

81

You Are in Christ

The transformation from old to new is not always a smooth operation because the old fights against the new. Remember— you're a work in progress. Some things like self-centeredness, gossip, or a critical spirit can be a struggle because they keep sneaking back into your life, a little at a time. If you think a little gossip, or a little time spent with someone who tempts you into bad behavior, or a little bit of something that you know in your heart will become addictive is not a problem ... you're wrong.

When you came into Christ you became a new person and those old behaviors must be replaced with new, Christ-honoring, Christ-pleasing behavior. Don't leave the door open even a crack to allow sins to sneak back in. Shut the door on the old. Open the door for the new.

Some things don't need to be cut back. They need to be cut off.
BETH MOORE

In His kindness God called you to share in His eternal glory by means of Christ Jesus. So after you have suffered a little while, He will restore, support, and strengthen you, and He will place you on a firm foundation.

1 PETER 5:10

82

You Are Restored

You are not alone. Jesus promised to be with you always. Yes, life will be hard sometimes but regardless of what you are going through and no matter how you feel; you are not alone. Things might get so messy that you wonder if God is paying attention or you may feel that He isn't helping at all. All your support systems could be torn down. You may even suffer because of your faith in Jesus. Don't give up!

Be encouraged by God's promises that none of this will last forever. He hasn't deserted you. He promises to support you and eventually set your feet on solid ground. These times of difficulty are when you need to keep the faith. Let your faith grow in difficult times by never doubting Him. Keep calling on Him and trusting Him, no matter what.

No matter what you're going through there is no pit
so deep that God can't reach in and get you out.

JOYCE MEYER

Dear friends,
we are already God's children,
but He has not yet shown us
what we will be like when
Christ appears.
But we do know that we
will be like Him,
for we will see Him
as He really is.

1 John 3:2

83

You Have Good Days and Hard Days

Let's be honest. Some days are good. Some days you think about others more than yourself. Some days you are kind and courteous to store workers. Some days you're patient with the kids. Some days start with Bible reading, prayer, and silence before God. Some days. Other days ... you're a mess, even if your intentions are good.

Don't beat yourself up. God isn't finished with you yet. You are a work in process. There will be good days and not-so-good days and that's OK. Don't get discouraged. Your heart's desire is definitely to know Jesus and live for Him but you're still working from a human body in a fallen world with Satan constantly working against you. God knows all that. He sees your heart's desire. He knows that when you do actually see Jesus, you will instantly be like Him. All that He's been teaching you will be accomplished!

Being a Christian is more than just an instantaneous conversion—it is a daily process whereby you grow to be more and more like Christ.

BILLY GRAHAM

Now may our
Lord Jesus Christ Himself,
and God our Father,
who *loved* us and gave us
eternal *comfort* and *good hope*
through *grace,*
comfort your hearts and establish
them in every
good work
and *word.*

2 Thessalonians 2:16-17

84

You Are Comforted

What does a child most want when she is hurt or scared? She wants to snuggle on the lap of a trusted adult who will hug her and tell her that everything is going to be all right. She wants her booboo kissed and to hear that the pain will go away. She wants diversion so the bad dream can be forgotten and the promise that her adult is protecting her. Comfort.

Everyone wants comfort when the storms of life are raging and there doesn't seem to be a solid foundation anywhere. You're promised comfort and peace. Comfort that's trustworthy because it comes from Jesus. No one loves you more. No one can see the bigger picture better. No one has a better plan for you than Jesus. Read His Word and find comfort there. Find comfort in the peace He settles in your heart. Trust Him. He loves you so very much.

You don't have to be alone in your hurt! Comfort is yours.
Joy is an option. And it's all been made possible by your Savior.
He went without comfort so you might have it. He postponed
joy so you might share in it. He willingly chose isolation
so you might never be alone in your hurt and sorrow.

JONI EARECKSON TADA

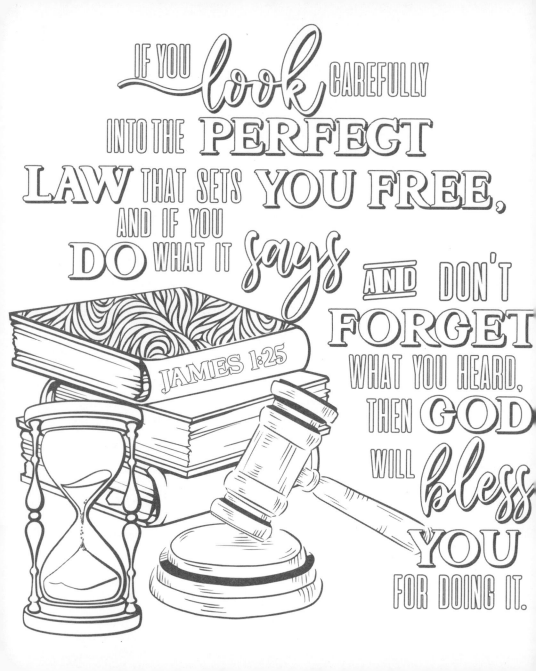

85

You Are Intentional

What does it mean to be blessed? It's being in a state of happiness or well-being. God blesses you if you pay attention to His Word. That matters because it tells you how to live in obedience to Him. It tells you how to get along with other people. It tells you which things are good to do and which are not. It's all laid out for you. All you have to do is read it with intentionality—pay close attention to what it says. Incorporate its teachings into how you live, not just out of obligation but because you choose to obey God and live for Him.

You aren't simply obeying rules so you'll be in good standing with God but you're doing what He says because you believe it gives you a better life and better relationships with other people.

Every Christian who does not study,
really study, the Bible every day is a fool.
R. A. TORREY

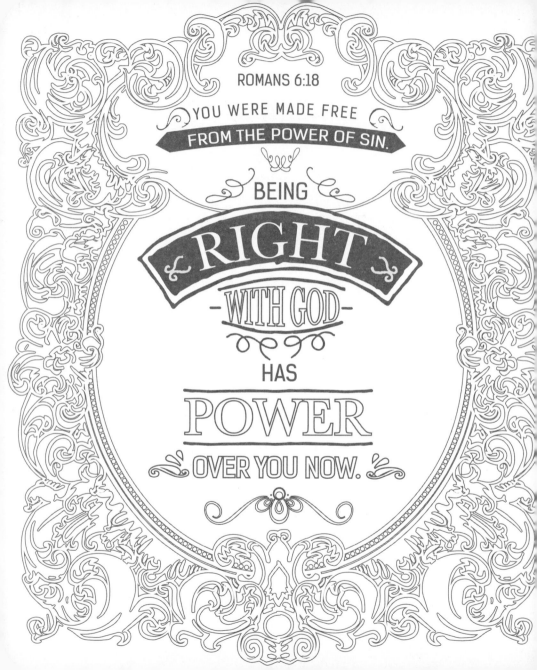

86

You Chose Well

From the first day that you could make a conscious choice about anything, sin had power over you. You chose it. Oh, probably not what people think of as terrible "big" sin, but sin just the same. Now, you may think that you are an independent person and not under anyone's power but you would be wrong. A person either chooses to serve God or to serve sin. Not to choose is still to choose.

Since you accepted Jesus as your Savior you have a relationship with God which means that you're now under His power. There is no better place to be. It may seem counter-intuitive but being under God's power actually gives you freedom because He loves you and wants the very best for your life. His power doesn't hold you down; it lifts you up and gives you the strength and wisdom to live your very best life. You chose well.

God always gives His best to those who leave the choice with Him.

JIM ELLIOT

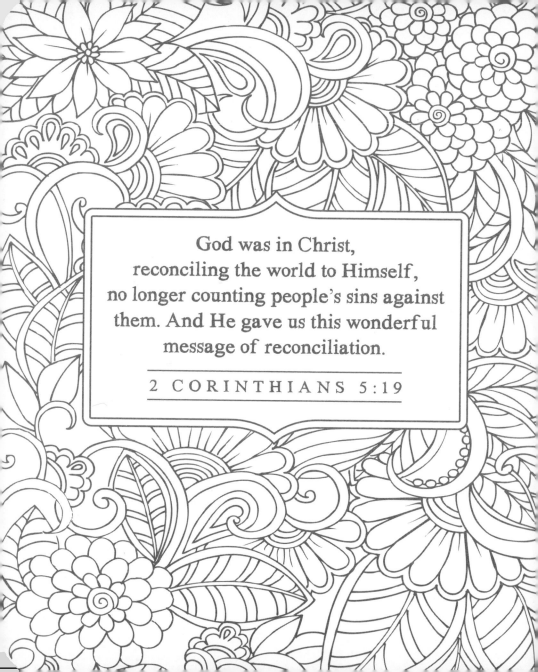

God was in Christ,
reconciling the world to Himself,
no longer counting people's sins against
them. And He gave us this wonderful
message of reconciliation.

2 CORINTHIANS 5:19

87

You Can Pay It Forward

God the Father and Jesus the Son were in agreement on the plan to provide a way for you to have a personal relationship with God. Their plan made a way for you to have access to the Father and was a direct result of Jesus' sacrificial death and resurrection. This changed everything for mankind since we started out one with God. But when sin entered into our experience we were separated from Him.

Reconciliation means mankind was able to come back into God's family and be with Him again. You are blessed to be able to pay it forward by sharing His message of reconciliation—the privilege of a God-relationship with others. That's what He wants you to do because He loves and loves and loves. He wants everyone to have the opportunity to know Him and you can help! You're not in this life alone—share the blessing.

Have you no wish for others to be saved?
Then you're not saved yourself, be sure of that.

CHARLES SPURGEON

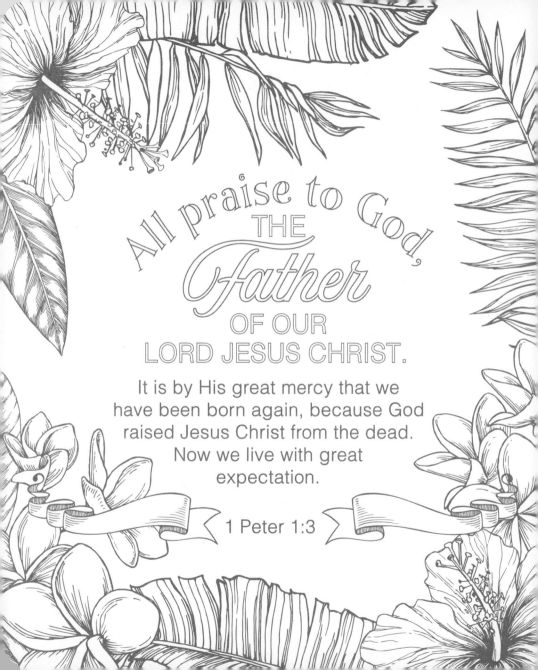

All praise to God, THE *Father* OF OUR LORD JESUS CHRIST.

It is by His great mercy that we have been born again, because God raised Jesus Christ from the dead. Now we live with great expectation.

1 Peter 1:3

88

You Have Hope

Hope is a beautiful thing. The underwhelming times in life filled with overwhelming struggles are when you need solid hope that things will get better. They will. The God you trust has power over everything and strength that is unmatched. You serve a God who makes promises and keeps them.

His power is seen by what He does—not only by His words. After all, actions speak louder than words. He loved so much that He sent His Son to die for your sins. His power blew death away when He raised Jesus back to life—there's your hope! His power cannot be stopped by anything. It's bigger than storms, evil, sickness, even death. You have an incredible hope that whatever you're struggling with, He can overcome it. Not only can He ... He will. Thank Him! Praise Him! Shout His glory from the rooftops! Share that unmatched hope!

May God remind us daily—no matter what kind of obstacles we face—that we are loved and empowered by the One who brought the universe into existence with the mere sound of His voice. Nothing is impossible for Him.

BETH MOORE

When
you became a

Christian,

you were set free from the sinful things of the world.
This was not done by human hands.

You were

set free

from the sins of your old self
by what was done in

Christ's body.

Colossians 2:11

89

You Answer to God

When you join a club there are often things you must do—initiations or dues you must pay. It costs you something to belong. Those costs or obligations are determined by the people who make the rules and set the price to be a part of their group. But when you became a Christian, a member of God's family, there were no initiation rituals, monthly dues, and man-made rules for you to adhere to.

Nope, nothing related to becoming a Christian is tainted by other humans. Jesus paid the price for your sin. He built the bridge for you to cross into a relationship with God. His words in Scripture are the guidelines for how to live. It's all Jesus. You only need to answer to Him as you obey His Word and pay attention to His Holy Spirit's leading.

Every time you open up your heart in obedience to God and worship Him with all your heart, all your mind, and all your soul, our beautiful Lord responds with His magnificent presence.

DARLENE ZSCHECH

THEY SANG A NEW SONG, SAYING,

"Worthy are You to take the scroll and to open its seals,
for You were slain, and by Your blood You ransomed people
for God from every tribe and language and people and nation,
and You have made them a kingdom and priests to our God,
and they shall reign on the earth."

REVELATION 5:9-10

90

You Are a Priest

Old Testament priests were chosen from the tribe of Levi and were set apart from average people. They had access to God. They were the only ones allowed in the Holy of Holies where the Ark of the Covenant, God's physical presence, rested.

The priests were the people's pipeline to God. That all changed when Jesus died. He ransomed all people—you! He gave you direct access to God anytime you want and anywhere you are. You don't need a priest to pray your words or offer your sacrifice. You are now a priest with the responsibility to share the news of Jesus' death and resurrection. You can tell others how to know God. You are "set apart" as a child of God but not set away from those who don't yet know. Share the good news—bring more priests into the kingdom!

If you had the cure to cancer, wouldn't you share it?
You have the cure to death ... get out there and share it!

KIRK CAMERON